102
GOOFY
Jokes

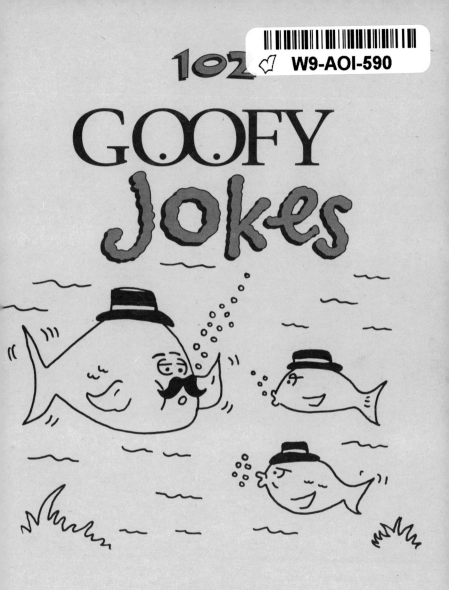

Morgan Matthews

Troll

This edition published in 2000.

Printed in the United States of America.

10   9   8   7   6   5

Where do tired trout sleep?

In riverbeds.

What do pilot rabbits fly?

Hare planes.

What's made of snow and is very sticky?

An ig-glue (igloo).

Why was the general in debt?

He charged too much.

What did the dryer say to the washer?

Let's go for a spin.

**What weapon goes buzz! buzz! when you
pull the trigger?**

A *beebee* gun.

Which dinosaur was really unlucky?

Tyrannosaurus *Hex*.

What sound does a 24-carat phone make?

It has a gold ring.

What has wings and solves number problems?

A *moth*ematician.

How do you mail a fence?

Use the fence post.

What did the plumber say to the noisy radiator?

Hey! Pipe down!

What do snowmen drink in the morning?

Freeze-dried coffee.

What do geese do in a traffic jam?

They honk a lot.

How do vegetables get around in the city?

They ride in taxi *cab*bages.

Which fruit tree is always grumpy?

The crab-apple tree.

Who was the fastest runner in history?

Adam. He was first in the human race.

Which jungle animal is always pouting?

The *whi*noceros.

Why was Miss Cow upset?

Her boyfriend was in a bullfight.

What did the farmer say to the seed?

I'll cheer for you if you'll root for me.

What's black and white and blue?

A very cold zebra.

Which monkey can fly?

A hot-air baboon.

Why are cars such a risky investment?

You can't stop them without breaking (braking) them.

Who is the oldest vegetable?

Pop Corn.

What did the ship say when it saw a floating marker?

Oh buoy!

What did the barbell say to the body builder?

How about a lift, pal?

Why didn't the little goat want to go to school?

He was the smallest kid in his class.

What do train conductors wear around their necks?

Railroad ties.

Why are turkeys so good at fixing shoes?

They do a lot of cobbling (gobbling).

How do you stop an olive from squeaking?

Use olive oil.

Why couldn't the flower ride its bike?

It lost its petals.

Why couldn't the duck buy a house?

He didn't have a down payment.

What do you call a happy baby sheep?

A merry little lamb.

How did the animal trainer get squashed?

He was teaching an elephant to lie down and roll over.

What fish sleeps in a portable bed?

The *cot*fish (codfish).

**What did the police officer say to
the octopus gangster?**

Throw down your arms!

What kind of car has whiskers and purrs?

A *Catillac*.

Where does a baby ear of corn sleep?

In a corncrib.

**Why did the businessman wear a bathing suit
to work?**

He rode to the office in a car-pool.

What has wheels and buzzes around the ceiling?

A *fly*cycle.

**What does a lumberjack use after the
A-Saw and the B-Saw?**

A C-Saw (seesaw).

Why was the bathtub exhausted?

It was drained.

What does Sergeant Needle have on his sleeves?

Pinstripes.

What did the waiter say to the skunk?

Sorry. I can't take your odor, sir.

Why did the artist go to the well?

He wanted to draw water.

How did the flame get away from the water?

It used a fire escape.

Where do cowboys bury their old shoes?

In Boot Hill.

Where do young locomotives go in the summer?

To *train*ing camp.

What do you call a person who sells tires?

A wheel-estate dealer.

What do burglars like to read?

*Crook*books (cookbooks).

Which vegetable ran in the Kentucky Derby?

The horseradish.

What kind of soup needs mouthwash?

Bad broth.

Where did the sick ship go?

To see a dock!

What do you call a person from New England who draws funny pictures?

A Yankee Doodler.

What do butterflies use to play catch?

A mothball.

What is a foot doctor's favorite song?

"There's No Business Like Toe Business."

Why couldn't the egg lend the rooster any money?

It was broke.

What happened to the house's chimney?

It flue away.

What did Judge Gopher say to Witness Mole?

Please tell the hole truth.

What did the ocean say to the muddy river?

Close your dirty mouth!

What did the goose say to the waiter?

Please put the check on my bill.

When do you have to pay extra for a rug?

When the charge includes carpet tax (tacks).

Where's the best place to buy a submarine?

At a sub (sandwich) shop.

Why do rabbits make bad leaders?

They have too many hare-brained schemes.

Which vegetable is in charge of the produce company?

Mr. Cabbage. He's the head man.

What did one wheel say to the other?

I tire easily. How about you?

Why did the lumberjack take his broken chopper to the hospital?

It needed an ax ray.

What does a kitten use to fix its fur?

A *cata*comb.

What did Mrs. Vegetable put in Mr. Vegetable's dress shirt?

Cornstarch.

What do you do if a bike commits a crime?

Put it behind handlebars.

Why did the gangster go to the dentist?

He had *crook*ed teeth.

What has big ears and lives in the mountains?

A mouse trapper.

What kind of shoe talks too much?

One with a wagging tongue.

What did the doctor say to the glue?

Stick out your tongue.

What did the wigmaker say to Shakespeare?

Toupee or not toupee.

**What do you call a pachyderm who lives in
Los Angeles, California?**

An L.A. Phant (elephant).

Which batteries always frown?

The ones with negative attitudes.

How did the river hurt itself?

It had a water*fall*.

Why did the fortune teller go to Hawaii?

She wanted to read some palm trees.

What kind of furniture is real cool and likes pop music?

The rockin' chair.

Why was the daisy farmer mad?

Because everything was coming up roses.

What kind of weather is a mistake?

Blunder and lightning.

Why did the cave get into trouble?

It had a big mouth!

Where do King Deer and Duke Pig live?

In Buck and Ham (Buckingham) Palace.

What has a beak and earns merit badges?

An eagle scout.

Why did the farmer call a doctor?

His corn had an earache.

**Why did the man take a pan to the
lottery drawing?**

He was hoping he'd have potluck.

What do you find on the floor of a dance studio?

Waltz-to-waltz carpeting.

Who is in charge of the forest?

The branch manager.

What did the police officer say to the turtleneck sweater?

Hey you! Pullover!

What kind of plant has teeth?

Chewing tobacco.

What do little frogs use to go fishing?

Tadpoles.

Who is the boss of the fish gangsters?

The *Cod*father (Godfather).

Where do you find a successful garbage man?

At the top of the heap.

**What does a locomotive have on the sides
of its head?**

Engine ears.

How can you make a car cry?

Turn on the windshield weepers (wipers).

What freshens your breath and goes toot toot?

A tuba toothpaste.

What do snowmen like to eat for supper?

Frozen dinners.

Why was the man's house full of rabbits?

He had central hare conditioning.

What kind of pants do ghosts wear?

*Boo*jeans.

Why did the reporter go to the ice-cream store?

He needed a scoop.

What spins and keeps good time?

A top (stop) watch.

What did the rope say to Tarzan?

I'm vine, how are you?